HOW TO STAY SANE AND SUCCESSFUL IN THE COVID WORLD

THRIVE, FLOURISH, AND PROSPER EVEN WHEN ALL THE RULES HAVE CHANGED

The book is dedicated to all those people who attended my first pilot as you provided me with the support and encouragement I needed to move forward with this project.

Copyright © 2020 Kathryn Mayer.
All rights reserved.
ISBN: 9781935059004

CONTENTS

"Disruption Introduction": The World Changed Overnight ... 5

CHAPTER 1:
Break Through the Panic or
Fight-Or-Flight Reaction by Taking Very Small Steps ... 11

CHAPTER 2:
Increase Experimenation in the Way that is Most Comfortable for you ... 15

CHAPTER 3:
Nurture yourself so you can bounce back more quickly ... 23

CHAPTER 4:
Exercise Your Network – The Final Frontier to Managing the Fear ... 31

Wrap-up ... 37

More Help From Kathryn ... 39

Endnotes ... 41

"Disruption Introduction": The World Changed Overnight

Feeling unsure about our choices might be "the new normal."

As we try to cope with the global pandemic, a shrunken economy, and a renewed focus on racial inequality all at once, organizations are struggling to figure out the right thing to do.

Because I facilitate groups for leaders, I know we must offer and create a safe space for conversations—as uncomfortable as that may be for everyone, including me. I do what I always do when I feel uncertain: reach out to my older and wiser mentors, and ask, "How can I be of service to people I'm coaching? What do people need now?"

The consistent answer was, "People need to be seen and heard right now. Just listen." I feel partial relief; I can do that, but it feels insufficient.

I return to work with a renewed commitment to just listen. I hear my clients expressing overwhelm:

- "I am feeling drained, exhausted…"

- "Everything is moving so slowly…"

- "Change is happening so fast…"

- "I can't achieve my usual stellar results. In fact, those large goals feel completely out of reach."

- I know I need to network more as my company's future seems uncertain, but how do you build relationships in the middle of a pandemic?"

- "I need my team to be innovative and come up with new business ideas if our company is to survive. But they seem focused on the old way of working…"

- I am losing resources, having to lay people off… and then three months later I have to hire them back! It is so confusing and frustrating…"

- "How do I motivate people when there will be no bonuses or meetings where I can bring their favorite donuts?"

- **"I am feeling out of control…"**

There's a consistent theme: everyone feels like they have lost control, had to abandon their usual way of working, and are confused about how to achieve the results they have grown to expect. Worst of all, there's no end in sight to the chaos. Whether they're highly seasoned executives or in their earlier part of their careers, whether they lead teams of half a dozen or hundreds, no one seems spared.

One of my clients, "Lisa" (all names have been changed), is usually the most upbeat and energetic leader of a large sales support team. She sounds exhausted and at her wit's end. Lisa works for a large retailer. She had to furlough a large part of her sales support team in March and now need to rehire and rapidly retrain them to new ways of working virtually as sales finally began to rebuild. Lisa had been a star performer, always exceeding her sales numbers and receiving overwhelming positive feedback from her team. As I listened to her describe her current challenges, the biggest obstacle came into focus: her perfectionist tendencies. She'd always been the perfect child, always received A grades, always outperformed and received the highest performance ratings. She always had high expectations for herself and her team. She thrived on setting and achieving lofty goals. Now, she felt completely adrift. How can she motivate others when she can't motivate herself?

I asked her what she was feeling. She said, "I feel like a failure." I asked her where in her body she felt like a failure. "I feel a real tightness across my chest." I asked her to take five slow deep breaths. This breathing exercise calmed her down and centered her. She was surprised how helpful something so simple could be. Her calm state helped her realize that she was beating herself up every day when she didn't achieve the results she'd been accustomed to expect from herself and her team.

Then I asked one of my favorite coaching questions, "How is that working?" It usually makes people laugh. Lisa smiled and said, "obviously, it is NOT!" I asked her what she thought might work better. Given all the challenges, uncertainty and change she was experiencing, might this be an opportunity to consider a new way of working? What might create a more motivational work environment? What motivated her? She loves to check things off her to do list—so maybe setting smaller, more achievable goals might make her feel better? She said she would experiment with this new way of working. Her new work mantra would be, "small goals, big wins."

As I reflected on my coaching conversation with Lisa, I realize how difficult it was for her to admit that she felt like a failure and needed help. Like so many others, Lisa had been successful and proud of her achievements and now was feeling at a loss.

In the midst of this epic set of disasters, some people advise, "turtle up," as reported in a recent article about why women struggle with networking during this pandemic.[1] Women want to connect—which is more challenging on Zoom—and the pandemic makes it easy to find excuses for not reaching out and asking for help. Might this crisis be our opportunity to work differently?

As we continue to navigate unchartered territory and must constantly pivot and adapt quickly, it's obvious how important it is to ask for (and receive) support and guidance.

Not all of us are as bold and brave as Steve Jobs, always ready to tell the world that it needed some bold new invention like "the computer for the rest of us" (original 1984 Mac), "1000 songs in your pocket" (iPod), or "a widescreen iPod with touch controls…a revolutionary mobile phone…a breakthrough Internet communications device… one device" (iPhone).[2] He said, "People don't know what they want until you show it to them."[3]

I would like to channel at least one tenth of Steve Jobs' mojo.

The Crisis Hits Home

On Sunday night, March 15th, just as the Corona virus is becoming a world-wide pandemic, my largest client emails me to cancel all live training for 2020. Overnight, I've lost close to 40-50% of my business. At least they're exploring some virtual training and paying me for the near-term cancelled programs. But as an independent consultant, I'm in shock! The recession has hit home. I have to scramble to figure out how to navigate this new world.

My first reaction was similar to most of my clients, to take control of what I can take control of. I start making the bed, which gives me a sense of accomplishment. Then, I get really compulsive. I continue to fuss with the covers to make sure all the sheets and covers hang an equal distance from the floor. I know this isn't the best use of my time, but I give into it. After five more minutes going back and forth rearranging the bedding, I feel satisfied. But even as I admire my perfect bed, I realize it isn't going to help me survive this crisis. I need a much braver and bolder approach.

For inspiration, I look around at my books and pick *In Other Words*, by Jhumpa Lahiri, out of the stack. A Pulitzer Prize winner, she's one of my favorite authors, and I'd recently heard speak about this book. It's her personal story of exploring the unknown and doing something that really stretched her outside of her comfort zone: learning Italian well enough to write a novel in it. Many people told her that it was a crazy idea. What so moved me about her journey was this paragraph,

> "Why, as an adult, as a writer, am I interested in this new relationship with imperfection? What does it offer me? Imperfection inspires invention, imagination, creativity. It stimulates. The more I feel imperfect, the more I feel alive."[4]

I thought, 'Wow! I want to feel that alive.' Right now, I'm terrified. I want to run or withdraw. I have no idea what's going to happen to my business. **I realize that if I'm going to succeed, I have to work differently: to move faster to create new ways to make money. I'm going to have to accept that I will make some mistakes. I can either feel anxious and awful or I can aim to be more like Jhumpa Lahiri and start enjoying the experimentation and imperfection.**

WHY IS THAT SO IMPORTANT NOW?

This virus has turned our world upside down, with a global health crisis creating a global economic crisis. But the virus also creates opportunity. Many entrepreneurs are adapting to the pandemic with new ways of working.

Josh Baron, an adjunct professor at Columbia Business School, said nimbleness is an advantage that smaller companies have over larger competitors. For example, one gym company that only worked in person has developed online options. A furniture company switched from mostly large-scale projects to making only small furniture that a single person can assemble.

Technology enables many of these changes. We can move processing of testing results to the cloud or have simple doctor appointments by video.[5] And the new COVID-19 vaccine is being developed rapidly by testing on animals and humans simultaneously,[6] which is much faster than the normal protocol of testing animals first. Organizations that can adapt quickly can still thrive. All of a sudden, speed and innovation are valued more than slow-walking toward perfection.

Why perfectionism limits your productivity during a crisis

So, what does productive mean in a crisis? **Doing great work is no longer enough.** Both QUANTITY *and* QUALITY are critical. Even perfectionists must complete some tasks 75% and not spend the extra effort to achieve 100%. Wharton Business School professor Adam Grant, in his 2016 book, Originals, says the trade-off between quantity and quality is false. Research shows new ideas increase quality. **But many people fail to generate new ideas because they're too focused on perfection.**[7]

The *New York Times Magazine* said we're now in the age of constant invention—which begets constant failure. Innovation's lifespan has never been shorter; most new products last just a few years, or less. **To harness this new age of failure, we have to quickly bounce back from mistakes.**[8]

So, what does this new way of working look like?

"DISRUPTION INTRODUCTION": THE WORLD CHANGED OVERNIGHT

WHAT'S THE NEW STRATEGY FOR SUCCESS IN DURING A CRISIS?

COVID-19 has dramatically changed our world's rules *and* values overnight:

IN THE CRISIS	BEFORE COVID-19
Moving fast and making it good enough	Going slower and making it perfect
Experimentation and reinvention; creating alternatives to the ways things have always been done	If it is not broken, don't change it. Or focus on gradual, continuous improvement rather than big breakthroughs.
Being human, compassionate, and humble	Being tough, seeking glory, and striving for more
Ask what constitutes success; don't assume you know. Investigate where and how can you help/volunteer beyond your usual responsibilities/role	Focus is on individual and team goals, rather than societal or organizational ones; becoming more siloed
Ask for stretch feedback, ideas, and support from trusted allies and outside experts who challenge your thinking	Build and expand your network to be more visible and understand the competitive landscape

My challenge, as a self-described "perfectionist in recovery," is to fully embrace that imperfection (not just a few small mistakes here and there) will be a new way of life. My self-worth has been tied up in having high standards. I **value being prepared and doing things well more than I do moving fast and doing something that's just good enough.** Therein lies the rub. I have to adapt to a new world where my long-held values aren't as relevant.

Speeding up and experimenting makes me feel incredibly anxious. It feels like driving 90 to 100 miles an hour in a car designed to go 60-70. **If I succeed in this new world, I need to learn to feel energized and excited by experimenting.** This crisis is an opportunity to increase my comfort with imperfection so I can drop into this mode whenever I need it. The next crisis may be right around the corner, after all.

Why this eBook?

This is your action plan: you'll learn to use this crisis to become more comfortable with experimenting and moving fast. If you're a perfectionist in recovery like me, and want to strengthen your ability to be at your best even if you're way outside your comfort zone, this is the book for you!

Perhaps you run a team or work in a large or small organization, or you're searching for a new job. The eBook will also help you survive this crisis by learning to work differently—and will include a few ideas from my forthcoming full-length book, *The Productive Perfectionist: A Woman's Guide to Smashing the Shackles of Perfectionism.*

What Results Can You Expect?

You will learn the SANE approach to surviving and growing during a crisis. As we go through the four simple ideas in the SANE formula, I'll share stories of how I and others use them to thrive.

THE SANE FORMULA

1. **Small steps:** Break both the "fight or flight" freak-out reaction and the perfectionist paralysis ("I can't do it perfectly, so I won't do it at all"), enabling you to move faster

2. **Accelerate experimentation:** Develop comfortable new ways of working, so you can expand your options, increase innovation, and enhance results

3. **Nurture:** Practice self-compassion, humility, and the idea that you and others can still grow—all of which help you recover more quickly from mistakes

4. **Exercise your network:** Ask people you trust for more stretch feedback and support than you would in "normal" times to ensure that you are moving beyond your comfort zone

CHAPTER 1:

Break Through the Panic or Fight-Or-Flight Reaction by Taking Very Small Steps

Negative emotions limit your brain's perception of possibilities, while positive emotions open us up to creativity and flexibility, say Doc Childre and Deborah Rozman in their book, *Transforming Anxiety.9*

When the COVID-19 crisis hits, one of the first people I call is my publishing consultant, Shel Horowitz. I'd been working for almost five years on my next book, *The Productive Perfectionist: A Woman's Guide to Smashing the Shackles of Perfectionism*, and am so close to finishing. In despair, I ask, "now, what should we do?" Shel enthusiastically replies, "now is the time to launch a new eBook quickly. Write it in 20 -30 hours. There is no time to make it perfect!"

As a recovering perfectionist, of course my first reaction is, "are you kidding me? When or how am I going to get that done?"

But, as I'm freaking out, I remember the jump-start advice a writing instructor gave me several years ago: aim for 30-minute writing shifts three days a week. So, I take a deep breath. If I take those sorts of tiny steps, I can calm down. And I can write that eBook (the very one you're reading right now). "Inch by inch, it's a cinch" became my new mantra…

First Reactions Quiz

I decide to pilot my ideas with a small group of trusted allies. I ask which of these reactions is most typical for each of them:

1. **FLIGHT/ESCAPE**
2. **FOCUS ON OTHERS**
3. **FOCUS ON SELF-CARE AND STAYING CALM**
4. **FIGHT/TAKE CONTROL**

Even though you're not in my pilot group, you can still answer ☺.

In the pilot, the two most common responses are escape or take control. One woman shared that like me, she makes her bed over and over because that's the one thing she can control. Another woman is bingeing on Netflix, while a man seeks solace reading 1,000-plus-page books. All the participants want to feel calmer and more joyful. How do we get there in a crisis?

Two Key Foundations for Staying Calm During a Crisis

Tiny steps are the KEYS to smashing the fight-or-flight reaction and moving you toward more mindful responses. Taking these small steps comes from two well-tested practices:

- **The ancient Japanese technique of Kaizen** (continuous improvement in small, incremental steps). Japanese corporations have long used the gentle technique of Kaizen to achieve their business goals and maintain excellence. Your brain is programmed to resist change. **By taking small steps, you literally rewire your brain so it bypasses the fight-or-flight response** and creates new connections so that you can move rapidly towards your goal.[10]

    Example: After the first session of the pilot program, a participant shared her new practice of spending five-minutes every morning writing down what she was grateful for. As a result, she was starting to feel more positive and beginning to look at her challenging work situation through a more optimistic lens. This tiny shift led her to consider new ways of working.

- **Taking small physical actions.** Research demonstrates that taking several slow deep breaths can reduce stress in the body and help to manage your emotions (instead of letting them manage you).[11] **You build new sensations in the body that are lighter, more expansive, and full of oxygen**—and that will eventually override the tight, heavy, constrained feelings of perfectionism and negative emotions.

    Example: While we practice social distancing and work from home, I've been spending more time exercising at home. I now hula-hoop for three to five minutes several times a day. It makes me feel silly and child-like, which is the perfect antidote to my serious perfectionist self. I'm always amazed at how five minutes of hula hooping can change my mood from feeling anxious or overwhelmed to light and relaxed—which in turn makes me more productive.

Mindfulness and Meditation

Do you have a meditation practice? Have you thought about it? This might be the right time to explore one of the many options, apps, and programs out there.

I'm a fan of Jon Kabat-Zinn's mindfulness mediation approach. He defines this as, "paying attention, on purpose, in the present moment and non-judgmentally. By focusing on the breath…it helps to manage pain, both physical and emotional. **The goal is to move from mindless reactivity to mindful responsiveness.**"[12] I continue to work on replacing reaction-based behavior with more thoughtful responses.

I practice mindfulness meditation in two ways:

- I have become more aware of anxiety. And, if I feel fearful or nervous, I slow down my breathing by taking five deep slow breaths any time throughout the day.

- I go for a thirty-minute walk every morning in a nearby city park. This is not something I ever did before. But I found walking a calming way to begin each day.

Moving from actions to habits

Actions turn into habits once you repeat them enough. There are a lot of myths about how long it takes to form a new habit. I used to believe it was 21 days, but recent research has found that on average, it took 66 days (more than two months). The range was wide: from 18 days—say, to drink a bottle of water with lunch every day—to 254 days to start running 20 minutes a day, 5 days a week.[13]

During a crisis, don't expect to be at your best. **You need to give yourself permission to make mistakes, to slide back to old ways—to perfect the new habit over time and not all at once.** It's totally normal to feel like you are faking it till you make it—because you're starting as a newbie. Every top achiever started as a clumsy beginner. Even the superstars in sports, arts, science, business, and every other field had to learn how to do it. You can't grow without some discomfort. Remember the first time you rode a bike—you probably fell down. A core driver of success is to learn how to be kind to yourself so you can bounce back more quickly. Throughout this brief eBook we'll provide options for you to experiment with adding some tiny actions to your repertoire with the larger goal of making them habits that could enrich your life for years to come.

How one health-care professional took tiny steps to calm

A client, a Ph.D. medical researcher, always places her patients first. During the COVID-19 crisis, she was under additional pressure—both professionally and at home. She realized that if she allowed herself 5-10 minutes between her endless Zoom meetings to take five deep breaths, she was able to stay calm and more positive. Each day, she told herself, "It is important to make time for self-care as that will energize me to solve larger problems." This led her to focus on small actions, such as mini-breaks and doing something nice for herself on a regular basis. The result was increased energy and creativity to devote to challenging work issues.

WHAT IS ONE SMALL STEP YOU CAN TAKE TO MAKE YOU FEEL SANE IN A CRISIS?

- Spend five minutes writing your gratitude list every morning and/or at the end of the day

- Take five slow, deep breaths several times throughout the day, between meetings, whenever you feel anxious

- Listen to music and/or dance to your favorite songs

- Spend 30 minutes tackling that challenging assignment and then do something easier

- What is yours?

CHAPTER 2:

Increase Experimenation in the Way that is Most Comfortable for you

"Never let a good crisis go to waste"
Attributed to Winston Churchill[14]

Things are getting weird. As this crisis progresses, I see my clients overnight start to act in ways neither of us would have ever imagined. **It seems as though the ones who are succeeding are the ones who can adapt the most quickly.** I realize that my clients are teaching me that I need to get weird, too.

As I listen to my executive coaching clients share their stories about how they are adapting to the crisis, I'm intrigued by their varied approaches:

- Jill, a senior executive who is very private and formal, shared that when she asked her team how they wanted to stay connected, they said they wanted to play weekly Zoom Bingo! This was way out of her norm but, much to her surprise, she said it was fun.

- Eric, normally bossy, had become very accommodating—asking his staff how they wanted to stay connected and get things done; he began having daily and evening check-in meetings.

- Delores, a C-suite leader who had previously spent her energy making her boss look good, had starting acting like an army general and was telling him and everyone else what to do after she'd been put in charge of the company's COVID-19 action plan.

I realize that **if I am going to succeed, I am going to have to work differently.** Meaning I am going to have to move faster to fully embrace this world of virtual learning and interaction.

I ask myself how I'll approach my experimenting, given that I'm frequently paralyzed by my fear of mistakes. Surprisingly, the answer that comes to me is to do what I've always done: seek out experts, watch TV news, read books about leaders, and get guidance from coaches, mentors, and valued stakeholders. **Getting support and guidance from trusted advisors gives me the courage and confidence I need.** I am not someone who naturally just jumps into something new without taking these tiny steps.

Over the first weekend in quarantine, I watch the CBS morning show and listen to Doris Kearns Goodwin speak about her book, *Leadership in Turbulent Times*. It's about four US presidents who led the country during times of crisis: Abraham Lincoln, Theodore Roosevelt, Franklin D. Roosevelt, and Lyndon B. Johnson. I immediately buy and read the book. What inspires me most is the chapter about FDR. Because he'd survived polio, he was quite the experimenter and he was willing to try all kinds of things to get out of the Great Depression.

And then - BINGO!

After listening to everyone discuss how I could help people during this crisis, I keep coming back to what my publishing consultant advised: now is the time to write an eBook on staying productive during the crisis, "but do it now!" There's no time for perfectionism!

Here we are. I am on my journey, writing the eBook—all my imperfections included. But the real beauty of all this is that **I feel more energized** and alive when I'm really honest with myself than I have in quite some time.

I'm a cautious Driven-to-Succeed (I'll explain in a moment)—yet, I'm broadening my approach to experiment and take risks. Let's review two key mindsets around risk-taking.

Two Mindsets Around Experimenting

A moment ago, I called myself a Driven-to-Succeed. The other type of mindset in this model is Driven-to-Prove. Let's explain the two mindsets so you can 1) better understand where you fall, and 2) develop tiny steps that make experimenting less scary for you and your team/colleagues.

> **Driven-to-Prove:** You have a high need to prove yourself and take on new challenges; your Challenge score is high
>
> **Driven-to-Succeed:** you have a high need for self-protection and for showing how you excel in your core competences, but find new challenges outside your core strengths uncomfortable, or even threatening; thus, you have a low Challenge score

In any particular situation, most people are one or the other; some straddle both. Most of us will tend towards one mindset—but over time and in certain circumstances, can shift. For example, someone who never hesitated to move to a new country for work

INCREASE EXPERIMENATION IN THE WAY THAT IS MOST COMFORTABLE FOR YOU

might become more conservative once he/she has a family. But that person still loves to jump into things, and finds ways to do that on the weekends. In contrast, someone like me, who is more cautious, may start jumping into new things more quickly as I become more confident over time.

(A little later, we'll overlay another pair of mindsets that give us even more tools for understanding and potentially changing our patterns. Stay tuned.)

Even though it will shift situationally, I begin my virtual SANE module by taking a poll and asking people to select their typical go-to approach around experimenting:

- I would rather jump out of an airplane than experiment!

- I rarely experiment unless I am forced to

- **I prefer to be prepared, test things, and go step by step**

- I like to experiment when the stakes are low

- **I enjoy jumping into things and seeing what happens!**

Driven-to-Succeed types will skew toward the middle bullet, while Driven-to-Proves will pick the last one. But perhaps because of this current crisis and the fear that has been elicited, the most common mindset among my pilot participants is the one in the middle: "I prefer to be prepared, test things and go step by step." A few people like to experiment, and a couple jump right in. The goal is to create awareness so you can comfortably stretch and move faster.

These approaches to experimenting are inspired by a diagnostic tool called the Birkman Instrument,* which explores how differences in perception impacts relationships, performance, and morale.[15] One component of the instrument, Challenge, measures the self-talk that drives behavior. We can see the behavior, but we often don't understand the mental messages that generate it. Challenge describes those internal messages.

---

* Background on the Birkman Method : When he enlisted in the US Army Air Corps and became a B-17 bomber pilot during World War II, Dr. Roger Birkman started exploring individual psychological differences. Dr. Birkman noticed that even though the pilots received the same training, they managed stress differently. Some pilots seemed to thrive when thrown into difficult situations, while others did not. The first iteration of the assessment was developed in 1951, and the version as we know it today was developed in the 1960s. The Birkman Instrument is designed to provide insight into what specifically drives each person's behavior—and using that insight to create greater choice and more self-responsibility. Numerous reliability and validity studies provide empirical support for its effectiveness. If you want to learn more or take the instrument, go to https://birkman.com/about-birkman/our-story-growth/ (verified June 15, 2020).

Driven to Prove versus Driven to Succeed

Over the past fifteen years, I've worked with Doug Leonard, an expert in the Birkman Method, to create two mindsets around risk-taking:

Driven to Prove—You have a high need to prove yourself and take on new challenges; your Challenge score is high

Driven to Succeed—You have a high need for self-protection and for showing how you excel in your core competences, but find new challenges that are outside your core strengths threatening or uncomfortable; thus, you have a low Challenge score

For both Driven-to-Prove and Driven-to-Succeed individuals, their identity is linked to behavior. **Whether our Challenge score is high or low, what we do is driven by how we create a sense of worth for ourselves. It's a continuum of mindset around risk-taking.**

Low (Driven to Succeed) . . . . High (Driven to Prove)

OVERVIEW OF DRIVEN TO SUCCEED

People who are driven to succeed act to protect their naturally existing positive sense of self (self-worth). They are typically confident of their abilities, pleasant, and persuasive. They take calculated risks based upon personal expertise. **They need to work on achievable goals where they can shine—and that receive praise/recognition to create an image of success.**

OVERVIEW OF DRIVEN TO PROVE

Those who are driven to prove are less focused on their image externally, yet they validate themselves externally by what gets done. Driven-to-Prove individuals are easily seduced by complex challenging problems and stretch goals—the harder the better. Strong-willed, determined, aware of personal shortcomings, **they accept greater risks—regardless of expertise—as a way to prove themselves**. They need to work with continually rising goals as an opportunity to demonstrate that they can handle challenges.

INCREASE EXPERIMENTATION IN THE WAY THAT IS MOST COMFORTABLE FOR YOU

WORKING TOGETHER

Driven-to-Prove and Driven-to-Succeed are complimentary. They share a common intensity to succeed. Each perspective has benefits. And some people see both sides. This means that are able to and can comfortably go back and forth between the two.

DRIVEN-TO-SUCCEED	SEE BOTH SIDES	DRIVEN TO PROVE
• Analyze *risk in advance*		• Analyze the *risk after the fact*
• Stretch your *core strengths*		
• Set *attainable* goals		• Focus on your *potential*
• Go *step by step* to ensure success		• *Continually elevate your goals* and focus on *proving yourself*
• Under stress—show a *positive image* to the world and *blame shortcomings on external factors*		• Under stress—become *critical of self and others*; sometimes *beat themselves up* even in public

EXAMPLES OF WELL-KNOWN LEADERS

Let's look at two successful leaders: A Driven-to-Prove and a Driven-to-Succeed.

Driven-to-Prove: Vera Wang is a world-renowned fashion designer. An English major at Sarah Lawrence College, she became the youngest editor of Vogue magazine. After 17 years at Vogue, she left to join Ralph Lauren. At age 40, she resigned and with no formal education in the clothing business started her own wedding dress firm and grew it to a multimillion-dollar company. She thrives on new adventures and succeeding against the odds.

Driven-to-Succeed: Mary Bara is the first female CEO of a major global automaker, General Motors (GM). She started her career at GM at the age of 18, right out of high school. She held various positions at GM in engineering and administrative roles and worked her way up the ranks to become CEO. She built her career moving step by step, leveraging her core strengths and adding to them over time.

Both Mindsets will Climb Mount Everest

You might think, 'it doesn't seem like the Driven-to-Succeed people really take risks. They appear much more cautious. Can they really think and go big?'

Yes! For example, two mountain climbers—a Driven-to-Prove and a Driven-to-Succeed—could both have a lifetime goal to climb Mt. Everest, but they'd approach it differently.

If their mountain climbing club planned a trip to climb Mt. Everest in two years, the Driven-to-Succeed would make sure she'd climbed enough small mountains and could manage the unique challenges of traversing that high; her goal would be to make it to the top. In contrast, the Driven-to-Prove would jump at the opportunity to join the trip, would get as prepared as possible, and wouldn't mind if she didn't see the summit. She just wouldn't want to pass up the challenge!

HOW THEY MANAGE STRESS

When things go wrong, their divergent viewpoints become intense. All of us want to champion our perspective, because it's strongly linked to our identity. How you feel good about you is in jeopardy. It's being compromised!

Think about a time when things didn't go well. How did you react? If you're not sure, ask a trusted friend or colleague.

- Under pressure, a Driven-to-Prove becomes extremely critical and demanding of self and others. The D-T-P feels inadequate, but is reluctant to accept success without critical review.

- A Driven-to-Succeed under pressure tends to blame personal problems or shortcomings on situational external factors (protecting self) and doesn't like public recognition of a problem.

WHAT EACH APPROACH NEEDS TO EXPERIMENT MORE COMFORTABLY

Driven-to-Succeed: People with this mindset need to experiment more, even if they can't predict the outcome. Here are simple steps they can take:

- Find partners/coaches to give a push and provide honest feedback/support

- Avoid taking the easy way out; continuously look for ways to improve

INCREASE EXPERIMENATION IN THE WAY THAT IS MOST COMFORTABLE FOR YOU

- Accept feedback without excuses and analyze it carefully
- Take more uncalculated personal risks

Driven-to-Prove: They need to be thoughtful before they plunge into the next experiment. Since not everyone is comfortable jumping in, they need to check in with others affected and determine what is realistic/appropriate for the situation by taking these steps:

- Find partners/coaches to rein them in/provide focus/be supportive
- Take time to calculate risks in advance before overcommitting
- Lighten up; accept and give praise without critique
- Be realistic about performance standards

HOW I, AS A DRIVEN-TO-SUCCEED, EXPERIMENT COMFORTABLY:

- Read books on well-known leaders, such as *Leadership in Turbulent Times* by Doris Kearns Goodwin
- Reach out to my publishing consultant, supervising coach, and valued clients. Get their views on how to help people and companies adapt/succeed.
- Increase time with my presentation coach for support and guidance
- Identify new standards of success that may not be about perfection

HOW A DRIVEN-TO-PROVE EXPERIMENTS DURING A CRISIS

- Make the experiments smaller—such as have Bingo games
- Reach out to a variety of people—include those with diverse approaches—to get their input, touch base, and see how they are feeling, as Eric the more controlling boss did
- Be transparent and evaluate performance standards—check in to see if these still motivate the desired results— and if they don't, recalibrate

- Share more about yourself that reveals your humanity: make fun of yourself, share your foibles

- Create opportunities for your team to meet informally (you have lots of options besides Bingo games)

WHAT SMALL STEPS CAN YOU TAKE TO EXPERIMENT THAT ARE COMFORTABLE FOR YOU AND THOSE AROUND YOU?

- Identify where you fall on the Driven-to-Prove or Driven-to-Succeed scale, and decide on an approach

- Ask your team/others whether they tend to jump in first or evaluate in advance and go step-by-step

- Seek out others who have diverse perspectives and gain their insights on your vision and possible actions

- Develop new definitions of success during the crisis—what is a win? What types of mistakes are permissible?

- Offer praise and specific feedback more often to those around you when they take small steps or take new actions

- Share your mindset around experimenting and what is challenging for you

- What is yours?

CHAPTER 3:

Nurture yourself so you can bounce back more quickly

"The art of life is not controlling what happens, it's using what happens."
And *"Limits lead to invention."*

Gloria Steinem[16]

Although I love these quotes, all I see is that my own limits are going to lead me to make more mistakes. Why is seeing opportunities for invention such a struggle for me? As a perfectionist in recovery, I have to continue working to overcome this feeling that my self-worth stems from accomplishments.

Or, as Carol Dweck, author of *Mindset: The New Psychology of Success,*[17] would put it, I've had a fixed mindset throughout my life, rather than a growthful one. And this is the other, overlapping mindset spectrum I promised in the previous chapter that we'd explore.

Dweck, a world-renowned Stanford University psychologist, has done decades of research on achievement and success. She shows that your view of yourself profoundly impacts the way you live your life: People with a growth mindset—**the belief that they can improve through their own efforts**—tend to thrive when things are not going well. And with that mindset, anyone can enhance their ability to play a sport or learn a new skill.

But if you tend toward a fixed mindset, you hold the belief that your qualities (such as math or athletic ability) are carved in stone. This belief tends to bring about an urgent need to prove yourself over and over again—which is what I did as a child tennis player. I felt that I was only as good as my latest win or loss, and that led to panic attacks during matches. **And in the fixed mindset, a failure just proves that you're not good enough!**

Fixed Versus Growth Mindset

IN THE CRISIS	BEFORE COVID-19
Your qualities, such as ability to do math or sports, are *carved in stone*.	You can *expand your skills through your efforts*; while there are differences in talents such as a math and sports, everyone can improve through practice and application.
Focus is on *proving* that you have a sufficient amount of these qualities.	Focus is on *potential*—stretching yourself even when it is not going well.
You feel smart when you *don't make mistakes and finish something fast*—and it's perfect.	You feel smart when you *try really hard and work on something over time* until you figure it out.
You *refuse to seek out criticism and ignore it when it shows up*.	You *seek out—and learn from—constructive feedback*.
Success is winning and showing your superiority; having to practice casts doubt on your talent. *Failure is losing; it's to be avoided*; you feel threatened by others' success.	Build and expand your network to be more visible and understand the competitive landscape
John McEnroe, former world #1 tennis player, looked to talent to carry him to success; when he wasn't winning, he *would blame others or have temper tantrums*.	Bruce Jenner, 1976 Olympic gold medalist, said he was successful because he had been dyslexic as a child—so he *learned to work hard to overcome challenges*.

Here we are in a crisis! Carol Dweck says that those with a growth mindset are most likely to thrive during challenging times like this. Why? *They focus more on making progress than on perfection.* **And they don't judge every mistake. Instead, they learn from it and move on.**

MY FIXED-MINDSET MOMENT

I had a challenging two days at work.

I facilitate two year-long women's leadership groups that had started pre-COVID and were meeting in person. Overnight, I had to become comfortable with facilitating on Zoom. And, I had to accept, as did the group, that we might not be meeting in person for quite some time.

Many of these women have small children, some have lost their jobs, and others have completely new challenges now that they are working at home and sheltering in place. My job is to help them grow as leaders and as people.

Pre-COVID, we met in person and had rich two-hour conversations with meaty exercises. Now, because their lives have become crazy with home-schooling children and working, they want to meet in one-hour blocks. I have two of these one-hour meetings in two days.

My facilitation is supposed to stretch them to think beyond the current world and grow their leadership skills. I wonder if a single hour is really enough to accomplish this. With this doubt in mind, I facilitate the first of the two sessions.

And the doubt starts to consume me.

I feel lost.

I feel I am not helping.

I feel I am stuck in the mud.

I feel out of touch.

I feel everyone is complaining.

I feel like a failure.

The next day, I reflect on these feelings. Pondering what can I do differently, I think about a comment from a program participant, Deborah, who had to confront her fixed mindset. She wishes she was back in 7th grade, where her 12-year-old son is learning about growth mindset in school. Things have certainly changed in school curricula since she and I were in school. *Deborah shares that she doesn't feel good enough right now*—and *that's exactly how I feel.*

I realize I'm not really embracing this challenge. I am usually energized by my experiences with these groups of women, but this COVID-19 situation makes me feel like I've signed up for combat duty in the army. I used to get to select and innovate in small ways. But now, I'm on the front line of innovation all the time—it feels like a frontal assault!

I watch some of Governor Andrew Cuomo's news briefings. He is most definitely on combat duty and on the front line of innovation 24/7. He continually says he doesn't know what is going to happen in regards to the virus—no one does.

Watching him, I realize I've been stuck in the Fixed mindset. And I also realize I don't have to know everything. It is all right to say I am not sure if this is working. And as I finally start being nice to myself, my negative feelings change from to possibility and opportunity.

The shift is certainly not instant. I still feel I don't have time to prepare properly enough to feel I'm doing things well. I still feel my failure to adopt quickly enough and feel confident. But I begin to notice that many others feel equally unsure and uncomfortable.

At the second one-hour meeting with one of my women's leadership groups, I declare I don't know and ask for feedback. I share that I don't want this to become a bitch session and I want to add value—but this is more challenging in one-hour sessions. In order to be kinder to myself, I share that this is a new situation for me too. I ask for their perspective and what they need to make this time valuable.

I feel a huge sense of relief. I am being compassionate towards myself and letting go of the feeling that I have to always be in charge and know everything. This lets me feel more connected to them—and to myself. Much to my surprise and delight, I get these comments from participants:

I am inspired by our conversations.
I have learned new ideas for how to cope with the current COVID situation.
I feel like you are our cheerleader.
I don't want this to become a self-help group and would like more structured exercises.
I want to keep refining my leadership skills and this group is helping me get there.
With a growth mindset, it is clear that I don't have to know everything.

I leave this conversation energized for future ones, brimming with new ideas I want to try and a sense of relief. This is what the growth mindset is all about—taking charge, asking for feedback. For me, it was taking a tiny step with a group that I felt I trusted. And my self-compassion facilitated my comfort with doing something so uncomfortable.

So, I revise my eBook to include the Fixed versus Growth mindsets.

NOTE: Whether you're Driven-to-Succeed or Driven-to-Prove, you can still find yourself exhibiting either fixed or growth mindset at different times

You might look at the definitions and think, 'I am fixed because I tend to avoid asking for constructive feedback.' Or, 'I like to prove that I can do something new, so I must have a growth mindset'. With a fixed mindset, you believe your abilities can't improve. But both kinds of Drivens know they can improve—at least when they're not feeling sunk. Driven-to-Proves believe they will grow best if they set high goals and jump right in, while Driven-to-Succeeds believe they can achieve anything if they go step by step. Both want to flourish, but see different ways to get there. And, unfortunately, depression, self-sabotage, and other negative emotions can knock either one off-track, just as I got stuck in a fixed mindset. Fortunately, that doesn't have to be permanent. Even after setbacks, you can still "get back on the horse," as I did.

What's one small step you can take to adopt a growth mindset to make you feel SANE in a crisis? Here are a few possibilities:

- Identify which mindset—growth or fixed—you're living in right now; don't judge yourself (a crisis can change everything)

- Start focusing on the effort you and others around you take, rather than focusing on evaluating results

- Offer positive and specific feedback regarding the effort that people are making, especially during the crisis

- Declare you don't know enough information or where this is going and ask for others' input

What's your next step?

Self-Compassion versus Judgment During a Crisis

People who experienced self-compassion were more likely to see their weaknesses as changeable. Self-compassion — far from taking them off the hook — actually increased their motivation to improve and avoid the same mistake again in the future.

Heidi Grant Halvorson[18]

Hearing that NYC residents might be placed under quarantine, I immediately text my hairdresser, Robin. The thought of my roots showing and my hair ballooning into a messy mop frightens me more than getting the Coronavirus. I have big, frizzy hair. Without proper care, I can look like a merino sheep connected to a power socket. Happily, if a bit sheepishly, I get my hair cut and colored—and feel beautiful. Robin assured me that wanting to look good during a crisis is perfectly normal. And I could adopt Robin's thinking! As we head into quarantines and possibly worse, it's really OK to ask, "What do we need to care for ourselves?"

The next day, one of my coaching clients begins the conversation by sharing that she feels guilty about wanting to get her hair blown out. She also has big, frizzy hair—and has an important virtual meeting coming up. She's fearful of what she will look like if she doesn't get her hair done beforehand.

We explore the way her self-talk tells her to focus on others more than herself; otherwise, she's being selfish. And she's judging herself negatively for having needs.

"Yes, things are bad here", she says, "But places like Syria are in much worse shape. They lack a lot of the necessities we all take for granted—running water, safe home, food, and sanitary living conditions."

Of course, my immediate reaction is guilt: people are dying and all I can care about is my hair? Why should I fret about my roots when my and others' lives could be at risk? What right do I have to have needs? What *really* matters at this time of uncertainty?

But as we continue the conversation, my client realizes that it would energize and anchor her to get her hair done. She agrees to call her hairdresser and see her before the quarantine if possible. She breathes a sigh of relief and feels better. And I realize I can also relax about getting my hair done.

This is what self-compassion feels like: Giving yourself a break and acknowledging your needs as valid. Even one small action can make you feel better. This small step provided my client with energy for bigger and more challenging actions she needed to take. It created positive feelings that allowed fresh creative thinking, which is what we need most during uncertain times.

SELF-ESTEEM – "I AM AWESOME"	SELF-COMPASSION – "TO ERR IS HUMAN" [19]
• Focus on building up and protecting self-esteem	• Focus on improving—or avoiding a similar mistake in the future
• Weaknesses are threats and create anxiety	• Non-evaluative: based in kindness and acceptance
• Evaluative: good or bad	• Increases well-being and optimism; *more likely to achieve goals*
• Useful for being courageous and influencing others—*but does not predict greater success*	

Of course, **self-esteem is still necessary.** We still need to be able to pound our chests and go for it. In a crisis, most of us are out of our comfort zones more often. Developing increased self-compassion will help you stay more positive. The optimist's growth mindset will help you stay calmer and less fearful and take tiny steps, as we discussed in the first chapter.

HERE ARE SOME SIMPLE GROWTH AND COMPASSION EXERCISES:

1. **Before you enter a new or scary situation**, reinforce the growth mindset. You are learning—focus on your progress. Regardless of the outcome, you're good enough!

2. **During events**, quietly repeat a mantra that calms you down. For example, during the COVID-19 crisis, I keep asking myself what is the most positive narrative I can find, such as "I am using this time to grow and try new things."

3. **After a setback**, talk to yourself in a gentle and understanding manner: practice positive psychology. Martin Seligman, the father of positive psychology, has found that people who practice more of an optimistic rather than pessimistic mindset are more resilient. The optimistic mindset makes permanent and universal explanations for good events and temporary and specific explanations for bad events—which means the optimist bounces back more quickly from mishaps. In contrast, those who make temporary and specific explanations for success, but permanent and universal explanations for setbacks, tend to collapse when things get tough.[20]

	OPTIMISTIC	PESSIMISTIC
GOOD EVENT	"I am a confident and effective speaker."	"I can make a good speech if I have time to practice and prepare, which rarely happens."
MISHAP	"I am new to presenting on virtual platforms and will need to practice more."	"I am not a strong presenter and working virtually makes it even tougher for me to succeed."

As you can see from the examples above, the optimistic person is more likely to bounce back and adapt more quickly to a new world.

CHAPTER 4:

Exercise Your Network — The Final Frontier to Managing the Fear

"Anything that's human is mentionable, and anything that is mentionable can be more manageable."[21]

Mr. Rogers

One of my last in-person meetings before the shutdown was on March 7th with John, one of my high-potential executive coaching clients. Like the rest of us, John was struggling to figure out how to get his staff to adapt to the uncharted waters of this new world.

John was a little panicked and off his stride. He works in the mall industry, which had already started to feel the impact of COVID-19. He could see it was going to get ugly—and he was right. He mentioned that his team did excellent work, but he needed them to step up and bring him new ideas. **If they were going to survive this, he needed his team to become really innovative.** But he had never asked this of them.

We started discussing how he might have conversations with his team to increase innovation. I gave John very honest feedback about how his competitive style has limited his team members' ability to be creative. Because of our trusted relationship and his hunger to learn, he was able to accept the feedback and quickly begin trying new approaches. He realized his usual approach of command and control would not work. John would have to apply more of a collaborative style. He'd use brainstorming exercises. And he'd have to clarify his new expectations. He left our meeting back in step, brimming with new tools and tactics to increase innovation within his team.

I left that meeting realizing that if leaders want to continue to be productive in these unprecedented and uncertain times, they will need to seek out advice, guidance, support, and honest feedback. They'd have learn to manage the fear and be more intentional in the types of conversations they were having.

And as an executive coach, I had to think about how I can best help my clients (and you). What types of conversations am I having? Are they the right ones to help me experiment? Am I honestly seeking out candid feedback?

I asked my pilot group what types of exchanges they're having during this crisis. I gave them several choices:

- Ask for specific advice on an action plan

- Seek guidance on path forward

- Request general support

- Solicit constructive feedback on past actions

- Request stretch feedback to grow

- Seek new ideas

What do you think were the most common answers?
About 60% of the group sought out support and guidance. Around 50% have sought out new ideas. But only about 25% of the group is soliciting constructive and stretch feedback.

We discussed the results. Participants said it's a tough time to ask for honest feedback. Things are challenging enough; do you really want more bad news? But is that a good thing? One woman, an executive leading a large team, shared that her team gave her some tough constructive feedback and it would have felt better if she had been the one to reach out first. **Given that most of us are facing unchartered waters, we need to be more intentional than ever in our quest for new ideas and feedback.**

Developing a Strategy for Seeking out Feedback

As someone who is Driven-to-Succeed, it is a challenge sometimes just to mention things—which is why I love the Mr. Rogers quote. I know I need a push to help me manage and get past the fear. Let's define some kinds of conversations—and then I'll share my journey through the conversations I had with those whose advice, guidance, support, and feedback I seek—the people who got me to develop this eBook—and how I used them to push me past the fear. And you can develop your own path. **It's critical during a crisis to find ways to INCREASE the amount and types of conversations you are having.**

FOUR TYPES OF CONVERSATIONS

GUIDANCE: Help and advice specifically focused on how to do something or get through a challenging situation or make an important and potentially confusing decision.

ADVICE: A more general opinion about what you should do or how you should act in a particular situation.

FEEDBACK: Information that enables you to develop or improve your **current performance,** usually given after an event or performance or in a coaching context. This is NOT advice. Rather, it is based on observations and can be positive and focused on **developing your performance in the future ("stretch feedback")** or critical and developmental (about behaviors you can change).

SUPPORT: Agreement with, resources to implement, and/or encouragement to someone or something, because you want a person or project to succeed.

LET'S DISTINGUISH BETWEEN DEVELOPMENTAL FEEDBACK AND STRETCH FEEDBACK

Developmental feedback: Recognizes and addresses an area where you could improve your current performance.

Stretch feedback and advice: Helps you advance in your performance or career. It does not address a specific shortcoming in your current role; rather, it highlights areas (possibly unexplored before now) where you need to develop competence before successfully moving to the next level or to handling new challenges (such as those arising from COVID-19).

THREE-PART FEEDBACK MESSAGE

Observation... When you... or I've noticed/observed [part 1] + I feel... (optional) [part 2] + Impact... [part 3] because

Developmental Feedback: "When you don't return my email within a few hours [part 1], I get frustrated [part 2] because I can't complete the proposal without your input [part 3]."

Stretch Feedback: "I notice that you rarely attend networking events [part 1]. If you want to get promoted to more senior levels, you need to increase your visibility [part 2]. Senior people don't know who you are and they won't promote someone they don't know [part 3]."

Two other conversations: Support and Idea generation

Support: To gain reassurance that the step you are about to take is the right one. This can include seeking out a sounding board, positive feedback, and encouragement—before you embark upon the course of action, and throughout the project. If your attempt to gain support is very convincing, you may even find that the listener offers resources to make it happen.

Idea generation: To provide you with the wealth of ideas that will enable you to decide on—and follow—a course of action with confidence.

My Conversational Strategy

"People were 28% more likely to get a new job through weak ties versus 17% from strong ties. Weak ties are more likely to open up access to a different network, facilitating the discovery of original leads."

Adam Grant, Give and Take, page 47[22]

To survive and thrive during this crisis, I know I need guidance from outside of my intimate circle of friends and colleagues—from my "weak ties." Strong ties are our close friends and deeply-trusted colleagues. In contrast, weak ties are our acquaintances: people we know casually or we have met through our strong ties.[23]

Yet seeking this guidance feels scary; I'm not sure I want to hear what they have to say. They may offer guidance beyond my comfort zone. It feels like eating more vegetables and weightlifting. But I know I need to do this, so I force myself.

As I shared at the beginning of the book, one of the first people I speak to is my publishing consultant, Shel. I've known him for over 15 years and know he will stretch my thinking. But when he tells me I should write a new eBook, I'm still taken aback. I want to finally finish my next print book, *The Productive Perfectionist: A Woman's Guide to Smashing the Shackles of Perfectionism*. But he says, "An eBook will be a great way for you to smash your shackles of perfectionism. Write it in 20-30 hours. There's no time to make it perfect."

This is most definitely a push, a stretch, and a new idea. I start to freak out. How am I going to do this?

I need support. So next, I speak to my business coach, Marty. I've been working with her for a decade. She helped me restart my business and create a small, profitable executive coaching practice.

First, Marty reassures me that I'm in good shape, because I've been working virtually for over a decade. Second, she asks me, "how does it feel when you think about writing this eBook and piloting the accompanying program?"

I reply, "It feels very exciting! I feel energized."

"*There's* your answer." She reaffirms that I'm resilient, ready for this challenge, and competent to get past my fear.

But I still worry! Who will attend the pilot? Who will read this eBook? Is this even a good idea? **I reach out to a few valued clients and coaching colleagues for guidance and support**—and to test the idea.

The most significant conversation I have is with Natalie, who runs a coaching/training company. We'd done some work together. I respect her as a coach and a businesswoman, and I can trust her to be honest. She thinks the idea has potential and wants to help promote it. She encourages me to test it.

What do I have to lose? I run it by a few other valued clients and coaches, and they agree. Then, I realize that if I am going to succeed, I need advice on how to present the program. I need to get this done fast—so who can help?

Who else but Gary, my favorite presentation coach, would be the best person to help me give guidance? He can handle all of it: advice, support, and feedback to develop an interactive learning program. A former actor and playwright, Gary coaches executives on how to make memorable presentations. I've been working with him for over fifteen years. We are friends too.

I call Gary and explain that I want to pilot a virtual (online) support group program that will become an eBook. I want it to be engaging—and it has to be done fast. He declared, "sign me up!"

Lastly, I ask the ten people who attend the pilot. They not only offer their perspectives on what they find most valuable, but also give me new ideas. For example, Deborah, a public relations executive in the session, gives me the insight to add the Growth vs. Fixed mindsets to the program (and the eBook). Interestingly, Deborah is an old friend with whom I had lost contact. She lost her job recently and reached out to me—and now we're reconnected again. A recent article by Adam Grant, the author of Give and Take, described how these dormant ties—people with whom we haven't talked to in a at least three years—can be surprisingly helpful. Why? It is easier to ask someone with whom we have a shared history.[24] This rekindling of an old relationship gets me thinking, who else can I reconnect with? And this can offer valuable insights!

When I reflect on these steps, I realize that **the role of all these conversations is to move me past the fear of inaction.** Am I past the fear? Not yet. But I realize that I need to **keep forcing myself to have some uncomfortable conversations.**

For me, that means reaching out to more people, asking for stretch feedback and new ideas.

My pattern seems to be: Stretch—Support/Guidance—Ideas/Guidance—Guidance/Feedback—Support—Stretch.

WHAT'S YOUR CONVERSATIONAL PATTERN THAT GETS YOU TO STRETCH?

Can you take small steps like these to receive more stretch and development feedback, more new ideas:

- Ask your boss or mentor what actions you can take to help the business/organization succeed. How have the standards or expectations changed during COVID? How can you provide the greatest assistance to the organization?

- Reflect on what type of guidance and support you need to grow. Think of a time when you were most comfortable trying new things and growing: What made you feel comfortable—and how?

- Identify your strongest connections and ask them if they would make some warm introductions. Tell them what you are looking for; who do they know who might be useful? For example, an easy way to do this is to look through people's LinkedIn contacts and ask for introductions.

- Make a list of those people whom you know from previous jobs or school who would fit into the category of a weak tie or more of a dormant relationship such as a Deborah. Who did you value? Who might be worth reaching out to?

Wrap-up

"I don't know."

New York State Governor Andrew Cuomo

I remember when I first heard Governor Andrew Cuomo say "I don't know."[25] I thought, 'wow, how the world has changed!' In the past, Cuomo often seemed to lead with arrogance, rather than humility.

But after the first time I heard him say these three words, I noticed he was starting to say them often—and many other prominent leaders say these same words regularly.

This observation made me reflect on how I tend to avoid these three words unless absolutely necessary. Admitting what I don't know terrifies me: My body tenses up as guilt and shame start to dominate my feelings—why don't I know the answer?

When the COVID situation became a grim reality, I had no idea what was going to happen to myself, my family, my business, my country, or the world. And no one else seemed to have a clue either. While that seemed frightening then, it seems almost normal just three months later.

Because I coach and facilitate leadership development programs with business leaders, I feel it's my job to be strong and show others I know what I am doing—that I have things under control. I can show some vulnerability but I can't seem completely lost. But when people as smart as Governor Cuomo and Dr. Anthony Fauci kept repeating that they don't know, I realized it was actually appropriate—even important—to say it. Saying anything else would be lying.

This, of course, is a huge challenge for me as a perfectionist in recovery, I feel at my best when I demonstrate my knowledge. Admitting I don't know makes me feel I'm not good enough. I should know the answer.

In the COVID era, though, I have to accept that I can still be an effective leadership coach even when I don't have all the answers. That I am smart enough to distinguish what I know and what I don't. I remember hearing Cuomo saying he couldn't answer a question because he wasn't a medical doctor and that is not his area of expertise. By admitting his lack of expertise, he opened the door for others. I realized that if I could learn to let go of perfection, I could quickly and easily collaborate with others.

The first time I said those three words to a group of senior-level women leaders, I was anxiously expecting to be judged negatively. To my surprise and relief, the conversation went well. The women were supportive; they were fine with what I suggested and didn't criticize me. My fear-based catastrophizing cycle—I will get bad reviews and they won't hire me to lead more programs—never happened. Instead, the women offered another idea for the future. Wow! I don't have to know everything. In fact, the more I share my humanity and humility, the more space it leaves for others to do the same.

These days, I breathe a bit deeper when I say I don't know. Just this simple act relaxes me and opens me up. I spend less time worrying that not knowing what I am doing will be a disaster. Instead, I offer up "I don't know" as a question to the group. I focus more on listening to others than on worrying about how I might be perceived.

This is a HUGE shift. It feels as though the virus has finally allowed me to accept that my imperfections don't mean I'm not good enough. It just means that I don't have all the answers—no one does. I can share what I think—and what I don't know. And I can learn from others. These days, I use those three little words constantly. And I feel both more alive and more curious about others' views. One of my friends even tells me, "this virus may literally be saving your life." After decades shackled by my own perfectionism, I am finally beginning a new chapter in imperfect living.

THE SANE FORMULA: RECAP/CHECKLIST

1. **Small steps:** Break both the "fight or flight" freak-out reaction and the perfectionist paralysis ("I can't do it perfectly, so I won't do it at all"), enabling you to move faster

2. **Accelerate experimentation:** Develop comfortable new ways of working, so you can expand your options, increase innovation, and enhance results

3. **Nurture:** Practice self-compassion, humility, and the idea that you and others can still grow—all of which help you recover more quickly from mistakes

4. **Exercise your network:** Ask people you trust for more stretch feedback and support than you would in "normal" times to ensure that you are moving beyond your comfort zone

More Help From Kathryn

- Sign up for her monthly newsletter for all of you who are striving for your personal excellence and want to play a bigger game in your career and life without the nagging fears of perfectionism holding you back. Click here to subscribe to Kathryn's blog https://lp.constantcontactpages.com/su/A1NmP6T

- Hire Kathryn to speak, either in-person or over the Internet. She has several powerful motivational talks available on perfectionism, collaborative competition, and other topics. Click here to learn about Kathryn's seminars and webinars https://lp.constantcontactpages.com/su/u3DwuCr

- Sign up for one of the SANE four-part support groups that will be offered. https://lp.constantcontactpages.com/su/lQ5x5RN

- Want to get my take on your leadership challenges? Click here to schedule a complimentary 30-minute strategy session. https://lp.constantcontactpages.com/su/6hbhmur

- Get notified as soon as Kathryn's forthcoming book, The Productive Perfectionist: A Woman's Guide to Smashing the Shackles of Perfectionism, is available (you can even get an autographed copy—or get some custom-printed with your company name to inspire your employees or impress your corporate clients. Click here to learn about The Productive Perfectionist book release https://lp.constantcontactpages.com/su/r80RwVs

Endnotes

1. Caroline Kitchener, "Women ask for coffee, men tend to call in favors: Why pandemic networking is even harder for women", https://www.thelily.com/women-ask-for-coffee-men-tend-to-call-in-favors-why-pandemic-networking-is-even-harder-for-women/. Verified June 15, 2020.

2. https://thenextweb.com/apple/2015/09/09/genius-annotated-with-genius/. Verified June 8, 2020.

3. https://www.goodreads.com/quotes/988332-some-people-say-give-the-customers-what-they-want-but. Verified June 8, 2020.

4. Jhumpa Lahiri, *In Other Words*. Knopf, 2016, verified at https://www.amazon.com/Other-Words-Jhumpa-Lahiri/dp/1101911468/ref=sr_1_1?crid=13SZBSPT637PZ&dchild=1&keywords=in+other+words+jhumpa+lahiri&qid=1594389576&sprefix=in+other+words+Jhumpa%2Caps%2C207&sr=8-1, June 15, 2020.

5. Paul Sullivan, "Open to New Ideas in a Shutdown. Some entrepreneurs are adapting to create business models that may stick past the pandemic." *New York Times*, April 18, 2020, p. B7. Published online April 17, 2020 under the title, "'I Didn't Want to Shut My Doors': Businesses Find Ways to Survive," https://www.nytimes.com/2020/04/17/your-money/small-business-survival-strategy-coronavirus.html. Verified June 15, 2020.

6. Nicole Lurie, Melanie Saville, Richard Hatchett, and Jane Halton. "Developing Covid-19 Vaccines at Pandemic Speed." *New England Journal of Medicine*, May 21, 2020. https://www.nejm.org/doi/full/10.1056/NEJMp2005630. Verified June 26, 2020.

7. Adam Grant, *Originals: How Non-Conformists Move the World* (Penguin, 2017), p. 37.

8. Adam Davidson, "Welcome to the Failure Age," *New York Times Magazine*, November 12, 2014, https://www.nytimes.com/2014/11/16/magazine/welcome-to-the-failure-age.html, accessed June 15, 2020. Published in print as "Perdantoj Gajnas Losers Win," November 16, 2014, p. MM40.

9. Doc Childre and Deborah Rozman, Ph.D., *Transforming Anxiety: The HeartMath Solution for Overcoming Fear and Worry and Creating Serenity* (New Harbinger, 2006), p. 56.

10. Robert Maurer, *One Small Step Can Change Your Life: The Kaizen Way* (Workman, 2014) pp 26-28.

11. Doc Childre and Deborah Rozman, Ph.D., *Transforming Anxiety: The HeartMath Solution for Overcoming Fear and Worry and Creating Serenity* (New Harbinger, 2006), p. 9.

12. John Kabat Zinn, quoted in Robert Booth, "Master of mindfulness, Jon Kabat-Zinn: 'People are losing their minds. That is what we need to wake up to,'" *The Guardian*, October 22, 2017, https://www.theguardian.com/lifeandstyle/2017/oct/22/mindfulness-jon-kabat-zinn-depression-trump-grenfell. Verified June 15, 2020.

13. James Clear "How Long Does it Actually Take to Form a New Habit? (Backed by Science)," https://jamesclear.com/new-habit. Verified June 16, 2020.

14. https://best-quotations.com/authquotes.php?auth=15. Verified June 11, 2020.

15. https://birkman.com/about/. Verified June 4, 2020.

16. Both quotes from Gloria Steinem, *The Truth Will Set You Free, But First It Will Piss You Off!: Thoughts on Life, Love, and Rebellion* (Random House, 2019), p. 76, https://www.goodreads.com/quotes/10074892-the-art-of-life-is-not-controlling-what-happens-it-s. Verified June 12, 2020.

17. Carol Dweck, *Mindset: The New Psychology of Success* (Random House, 2006). The entire book explores the interplay of fixed vs. growth mindsets, beginning on page 18. https://www.google.com/books/edition/Mindset/fdjqz0TPL2wC?hl=en&gbpv=1&bsq=growth%20mindset. Verified June 12, 2020.

18. Heidi Grant Halvorson, "To Succeed, Forget Self-Esteem," *Harvard Business Review*, September 20, 2012, https://hbr.org/2012/09/to-succeed-forget-self-esteem. Verified June 8, 2020.

19. Heidi Grant Halvorson, *Ibid*.

20. Martin E. P. Seligman, *Authentic Happiness – Using the New Positive Psychology to Realize Your Potential for Lasting Fulfillment* (Free Press, 2002), p.93.

21. https://www.goodreads.com/quotes/157666-anything-that-s-human-is-mentionable-and-anything-that-is-mentionable. Verified June 12, 2020.

22. Adam Grant, *Give and Take: Why Helping Others Drives Our Success* (Penguin, 2014), p. 47

23. Ibid., p. 47

24. Adam Grant, "Reconnecting Opens Possibilities of New People and New Leads," *New York Times*, June 8, 2020.

25. Terry Sheridan, "Cuomo On Quarantine: 'I Don't Even Know What That Means,'" WSHU (NPR affiliate) radio site, Fairfield, CT, March 28, 2020. Full quote: "I don't even know what that means", Cuomo said. I don't know how that could be legally enforceable, and from a medical point of view I don't know what you would be accomplishing. But I can tell you I don't even like the sound of it. Not even understanding what it is, I don't like the sound of it." https://www.wshu.org/post/cuomo-quarantine-i-dont-even-know-what-means#stream/0. Verified June 11, 2020.

www.ingramcontent.com/pod-product-compliance
Lightning Source LLC
Chambersburg PA
CBHW070044070426
42449CB00012BA/3155